MY SECOND WORLD WAR

Daniel James

W

FRANKLIN WATTS
LONDON • SYDNEY

IN ASSOCIATION WITH

IMPERIAL WAR
MUSEUM

First published in 2008 by Franklin Watts

Copyright © 2008 Franklin Watts

Franklin Watts
338 Euston Road
London NW1 3BH

Franklin Watts Australia
Level 17/207 Kent Street
Sydney, NSW 2000

A CIP catalogue record for this book is available
from the British Library.

Dewey number: 941.084

ISBN 978 0 7496 7116 7

Printed in China

Franklin Watts is a division of Hachette Children's Books,
an Hachette Livre UK company.

www.hachettelivre.co.uk

Editor: Sarah Ridley
Design: Billin Design Solutions
Editor-in-chief: John Miles
Art director: Jonathan Hair
Maps: Jason Billin

With many thanks to Terry Charman and the staff at the Imperial War Museum's Document, Sound
and Photograph Archives.

Picture credits:

All images copyright © Imperial War Museum unless otherwise stated.

Front cover, clockwise from top: MH 034150, C 002433, D 2590, D011310, © Franklin Watts, D005937,
EPH 3270, D002614, HU 001135, © Joseph Reynolds.

Back cover, clockwise from top: MH 034150, D 2590, C 002433, D005937, D011310, © Franklin Watts, EPH 3270,
D002614, HU 001135, © Joseph Reynolds.

Insides: p1, pp2-3 HU 044973; p04 HU 001135; p08 NYT 007633D; p09 IWM FLM 002365 (top), H 041849
(bottom), D 2373a (bgnd); p10 D 003162 (top); MossmanEB 007526 1c (middle); p11 D 002222 (inset);
D 003162 (bgnd); p12 D011310 (ration book); IWM PST 13888 (poster); p13 D 002614 (top); D 002373 (insert &
bgnd); p14 NYP 068075; p15 MallowsLD 003315 2 (middle), HU 001135 (bgnd) p16 HU 001135
p17 © Joseph Reynolds; HU 001135 (bgnd); p18 MH 033883 (middle); CH 2926 (bottom); p19 C 002433 (top);
NA 011413a (bottom); p20 D 001568; p21 H 003978 (inset); D 001568 (bgnd); p22 D 005937 (middle); LambahP
0000243 1c (bottom); p23 © Penny Rowlinson; HU 036188 (bottom); p24 OEM 003597 (top); NYP 068079
(inset); p25 OEM 006631 (inset & bgnd); p26 A 005745; p27 A 004566 (inset); A 005444 (bgnd); p28 A 013370;
p29 A 017024 (inset & bgnd); p30 C 005102 (top), C 003729 (middle), TR 001129 (bottom); p31 HU 069915
(top), IWM FLM 002365 (bottom left); IWM FLM 002342 (bottom right); p32 CH 014235 (middle); H 038458
(bottom); p33 A 023938 (inset); BU 001181 (bgnd); p34 BU 003813; p35 BU 003783 (inset), BU 003813 (bgnd);
p36 BU 003807; p37 BU 003823 (inset), BU003813 (bgnd); p38 H 041849; p39 HU 049414 (middle right); TR
002877 (bottom right and bgnd); p40 RNY 075717 A; p41 HU 044878 (top insert); MH 029427 (bottom & bgnd);
pp43-45 D 001568; pp46-48 A 017024.

The publishers would also like to thank Joseph Reynolds and Penny Rowlinson for permission to publish the
photographs and accounts on pages 17 and 23.

III The Battle of the Atlantic   1939 – 1943

The German Navy had been trying to blockade Great Britain throughout the war and with the invasion of Britain postponed, the Battle of the Atlantic took centre stage. Two key questions sum up the third stage of the war. Could Allied convoys hold out against the threat from German U-boats? And would Germany's attacks on merchant shipping bring America into the war on the Allied side? It took the Japanese attacks on Pearl Harbor in late 1941 to do that.

IV The Battle for Germany   1943 – April 1945

It took the Allies over a year to gather their strength for the counter-offensive in Europe. Britain struck a morale-boosting blow with the famous Dambusters Raid in 1943, causing flooding in Germany's economic heartland. On 6 June 1944 the Allies returned in force to France with the D-day landings in Normandy. With the support of America and Russia, the Allies pushed the German forces back. As they advanced on Germany they uncovered evidence of Nazi atrocities far worse than they could ever have imagined.

V The End of War?   30 April – 15 August 1945

Hitler soon realised the end was near and, with Germany divided and overrun, committed suicide in his bunker. The Russians took control of Berlin and the Alllies celebrated VE Day on 8 May 1945. The war, however, was still not over. In the Far East, fierce fighting continued and it was only with the dropping of two atomic bombs that the Second World War was brought to a close.

Operation Pied Piper

Date: 1 – 3 September 1939

On 1 September 1939, Nazi Germany invaded Poland, which Britain and France had promised to protect. Britain immediately put its evacuation plan, Operation Pied Piper, into action. Children and their teachers, as well as mothers with infants, were hurriedly moved from major cities to the countryside where they would be safe from German air-raids.

The evacuee: Elizabeth Mossman was evacuated to West Wittering with other pupils from Ensham Central School in Tooting, London. She wrote this account:

" During the week before the declaration of World War II, I went to school each morning not knowing if I would return to my home at night. On the Monday of that week we were told to take a suitcase to school with clothes and any items which we thought we might need. We left our suitcases at school and then, on the morning of September 1st 1939, we went to school as usual, but this time we collected our suitcases and were taken to the station in buses. Each of us had name labels on our coats and we also had our gas masks in cardboard boxes...

My school was Ensham Central School, Tooting and I lived in Streatham Vale, London. We boarded our train not having any knowledge of where we were being taken.

At the Memorial Hall in West Wittering, the billeting officer and his helpers gave us the address of our hostess... I was sent with a classmate to a farm on the outskirts of the village... "

Elizabeth won a letter competition in the *News Chronicle*:

September 1939

Dear Editor,

I'm sure it was a surprise for all us evacuees to find ourselves scattered about the country, taken to a new home and getting to know our new foster mothers and fathers. At first it was just like another holiday but after a time a funny feeling of homesickness seemed to creep into me and I hoped and prayed that the war would end. But it was no use feeling down-hearted and if we evacuees do stay out of London, I'm sure we will be doing our bit for our country as well as helping the government. One of the advantages is the wonderful country air which makes one so healthy. Londoners notice a great difference in the atmosphere of both town and country. Country lanes and roads give place to the busy main roads and suburbs and transport is very different than in the town. Shops are few and if one lives quite a way from the village one has to make quite certain of stores and odds and ends. Round about here the village names sound much like birds – e.g. East and West Wittering, Chichester and a few others. Well I don't think I am any the worse for being evacuated, in fact it has been quite an experience.

Love,

Elizabeth Mossman, 13 yrs

Somewhere in the countryside – young evacuees lean on a gate.

War declared

In just three days, more than one-and-a-half million people were safely evacuated from major cities. At 11 am on 3 September, Britain declared war on Germany and braced itself for German air-raids. What followed was a period known as the 'Phoney War', with no German air-raids for another eight months. Lulled into a false sense of security, over half the evacuated children returned home to be with their families. Then, the Blitz began in earnest.

Food Rationing

Date: 8 January 1940

Britain was reliant on the large amounts of food, oil and other supplies, which came in by ship from America. These ships were vulnerable to attack from German submarines in the Atlantic. It soon became clear that Britain would have to consume less if it was to survive.

On 8 January 1940, the government introduced the rationing of bacon, eggs and sugar to provide fair shares of some foods. Everyone was issued with a ration book. These contained coupons that had to be used when buying a rationed item. Long queues and food shortages became a part of everyday life. However, restaurants and works canteens were exempt from rationing, so people who could afford to eat out or who had access to canteens could usually get good food.

Wartime ration books.

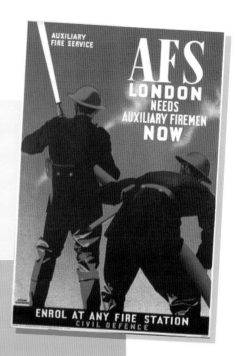

A recruitment poster for the AFS.

The hungry fireman: Francis Goddard was a fireman working for the Auxiliary Fire Service in Tottenham, London. He couldn't afford to eat out much, but luckily for him, his wife had another solution, as he relates:

Everybody had their crafty ways of getting extra food. Black market food. It was the only way you could survive.

AFS firemen in action, 1941.

My wife was working in a restaurant that had really good food – salmon, pheasants, turkeys, steaks, roasts – and whenever they got the chance, the staff brought things away. I got luxury food during the war, that I'd never had before. Fresh salmon, steaks, kippers – and she brought it all back in her knickers! When she was serving, she'd slide food into the extra pair of knickers she'd put on.

I had some fine meals at three o'clock in the morning. I'd be in bed and she'd empty her purse out and pour out the tips and say, 'Cor, I've had a good night tonight – I've collected over three pounds,' and out would come two nice pieces of cold cooked steak and we'd sit there and eat them. Or it might be a piece of salmon or some tasty sweet. She might even bring out a great big piece of chocolate.

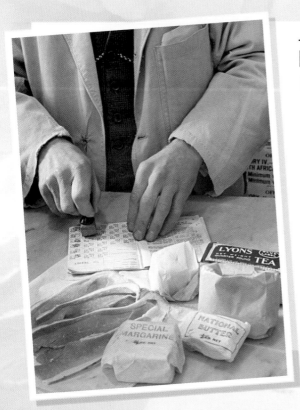

Rationing – a way of life

Rationing was not completely fair, as Francis' story shows, but it was vital in cutting Britain's food consumption and reliance on imports, allowing more resources to be focused on the war effort. Petrol and clothes were also rationed during the war and food rationing continued after the war itself had ended. It wasn't until 4 July 1954 that the last restrictions on meat and bacon were lifted.

13

A grocer stamps a food ration book during the war.

Operation Dynamo
The Evacuation of Dunkirk
Date: 26 May – 3 June 1940

On 9 April 1940 Nazi forces attacked Denmark and Norway; 10 May saw the Netherlands, Luxembourg, Belgium and France invaded. The British Expeditionary Force, fighting alongside the French, was forced back through France by the German armies. On 24 May, with Allied forces trapped at the port of Dunkirk in north-west France, Hitler gave the order for the Luftwaffe – the German air force – to finish off the stranded troops.

British troops queue on the beach at Dunkirk to await evacuation.

Time was of the essence and on 26 May, the British launched the largest sea-borne rescue operation of all time, Operation Dynamo. British Prime Minister Winston Churchill appealed for ships – even small ones – to join in the evacuation, pick up troops from the beaches of Dunkirk and return them to England.

A map of the English Channel, showing the locations of Dunkirk and Dover.

The HMS Princess Elizabeth *in a photo taken by Les Mallows.*

The seaman: Les Mallows, a seaman aboard HMS *Princess Elizabeth*, one of over 700 ships involved in the evacuation, wrote:

> The first unforgettable sight: six miles of beaches leading westward up to the distant port of Dunkirk, and this long stretch of light and sand appears spotted and blotched with small groups and larger formations of soldiers. The lorries, trucks and Bren-carriers which have got them there are standing abandoned around the dunes that lie along the top of the beaches, except where the smart white hotels of La Panne intrude on the scene.
>
> Along this seafront there are something like 40 ships, anchored as close inshore as their draught will allow. Naval vessels such as destroyers and fleet-minesweepers are mixed up with small merchant ships, trawlers and drifters, smart motor-yachts and a goodly number of paddlers. All their small boats are plying to and fro from the beaches, and as some ships move away with crowded decks, others like ourselves are constantly moving in to 'join the club'.

It was quite dark when the first of our two boats, rowed by a mix volunteer crew of seamen and stokers, grounded its bows close to the shore. Nobody seemed to be aware of their arrival and the Sub-Lieutenant in charge was surprised to find himself splashing ashore and groping along the beach for some time before he found a column of troops and led them back to the boat.

The first arrivals disposed themselves at the bottom of the boat between the four pairs of oarsmen; and soon afterwards they were being helped up on to the ship. And so we welcomed aboard the first soldiers that the *Princess Elizabeth* was to bring home from Dunkirk during that week.

Our second trip met a very different situation. Our arrival at the water's edge was now keenly looked for, but we grounded on a hump of sand some distance out. To the army, the prospect of having to do more than paddle did not appeal – especially with the greatcoats and slung-rifles that most of them still retained. Some persuasive hollering by the Subby [Sub-Lieutenant] in charge induced a steady wading-out, but within a yard or two of the boat, the water was up to their armpits and they feared any further move. The boat's crew got impatient, but the dimly-lit heads stayed put.

At last the Subby thought of shouting, 'Who wants to go HOME?' and this highly emotive word was only too effective. The nearest soldiers threw themselves at the shore-side gunwale, tipping the boat sharply on its side and throwing two of the oarsmen into the sea!

Some of the British soldiers trapped at Dunkirk await evacuation.

16

The soldier: Not all British troops were evacuated at Dunkirk. Joe Reynolds had two lucky escapes in the spring of 1940.

> My leave entitlement came up on 8 May 1940 so I went home. It is said that the sun shines on some people. It certainly shone on me that time. I reached home on the ninth and the Germans moved into Belgium on the tenth. I was at home to open the door to the telegraph boy and accept the telegram to say that I was missing in action!
>
> When my leave was over it was back to France. After disembarking at Cherbourg I wound up at Nantes in Brittany. About the middle of June, orders came through suddenly to evacuate to St Nazaire. I spent an uncomfortable journey perched on a flat-back lorry with nothing to hang on to, being shot at. Waiting on the quayside wasn't much fun either, as we were machine-gunned by enemy aircraft.
>
> We embarked onto two ships – a White Star passenger liner, I think the *Georgic*, and another liner, the *Lancastria*. I was lucky to go on the *Georgic*. During the night an enemy air-raid sank the *Lancastria*, which was lying quite close to the *Georgic*, with huge loss of life.
>
> We arrived at Liverpool the next day and then had a train journey to Leicester. We were dumped in a great big park. It wasn't long before the local ladies appeared, some still in their dressing gowns, with jugs of tea and sandwiches. The effort was truly appreciated. I suppose it must have been a reaction following Dunkirk.

Success

Between 26 May and 4 June 1940, more than 338,000 men were rescued from Dunkirk and the British army lived to fight another day. Churchill was quick to remind the nation however that, "Wars are not won by evacuations," and that there was still much work to be done to overcome the Nazi threat. The loss of the *Lancastria* was the single greatest loss of life for the British in the war – it is thought that 4,000 men died. News of the tragedy was suppressed for six weeks so as not to affect morale.

The Battle of Britain

Date: 10 July – 31 October 1940

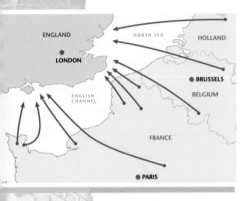

A map showing the direction of German aerial attacks on Britain.

After the French signed an armistice with the Germans in June 1940, Hitler turned his attention to Britain. From July to October 1940, a battle raged for control of the skies above the English Channel. Without air supremacy, Hitler believed his planned invasion of Britain, Operation Sealion, would not be a success. Wave after wave of air attacks by the Luftwaffe were bravely beaten back by the Royal Air Force (RAF).

The Spitfire pilot: D L Armitage was in No.11 Group, RAF, and flew a Spitfire during the Battle of Britain. He recalled:

"We took off, and after a time we came down, re-loaded and took off again. We lost our Commanding Officer after only a few days. He was seen to bale out apparently unhurt but his body was found as full of holes as a sieve... Our Wilkie, as we called him, was much loved and the thought that he was shot-up while dangling helplessly from a parachute filled us with a vindictive hate [of the Germans] which had not been there before.

In only another few days our senior Flight Commander got into trouble too, badly singed before he could get out of his blazing Spitfire, and so, in a matter of a little more than a week I changed from my position of junior Flight Commander to being in charge of the squadron...

A Spitfire as flown by D L Armitage.

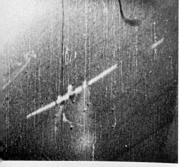
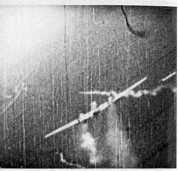

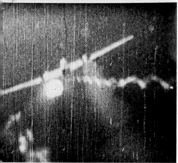

It was the evenings that got me down. We would return to our home base at dusk, tell our crews what repairs our aircraft needed and get a bite of grub. Then the lads would let themselves go. Some would go pub-crawling; some would seek out the local female attractions; some would stay in the mess playing darts and snooker and shove-halfpenny and discussing the day's action; nearly all would get a bellyful of beer before they went to bed.

But as temporary acting Squadron Commander, I would get down to the awful job of writing to the parents or wives of the lads who had not come back. For several days there was at least one to do every night. I tried hard at first, often tearing up two or three letters before I was satisfied. But I am afraid before the end I had developed a more or less stereotyped letter which needed little more than the name and address adding. This part of the job was indeed a harrowing one, but once you were back in the air it was all right. You had no time to think about anything but the job on hand and I believe many of the lads really enjoyed every moment of it.

"

This sequence of stills shows a German Messerschmitt Me 110 aircraft being shot down by a Spitfire.

The remains of a Messerschmitt Me 109 fighter shot down over southern England.

The battle won

During the Battle of Britain, 3,080 aircrew served in RAF Fighter Command, 520 of whom were killed. Despite the great losses, their contribution was decisive and meant that on 17 September 1940, Hitler postponed Operation Sealion.

The Blitz

Date: 7 September 1940 – 10 May 1941

Although the German plan for the invasion of Britain had been shelved, Britain was by no means safe. The Luftwaffe changed tactics and started to focus on bombing British cities, starting with London. Hitler hoped he could demoralise the British people and force the government to accept peace terms, but Prime Minister Winston Churchill was adamant that Britain would keep fighting until the end.

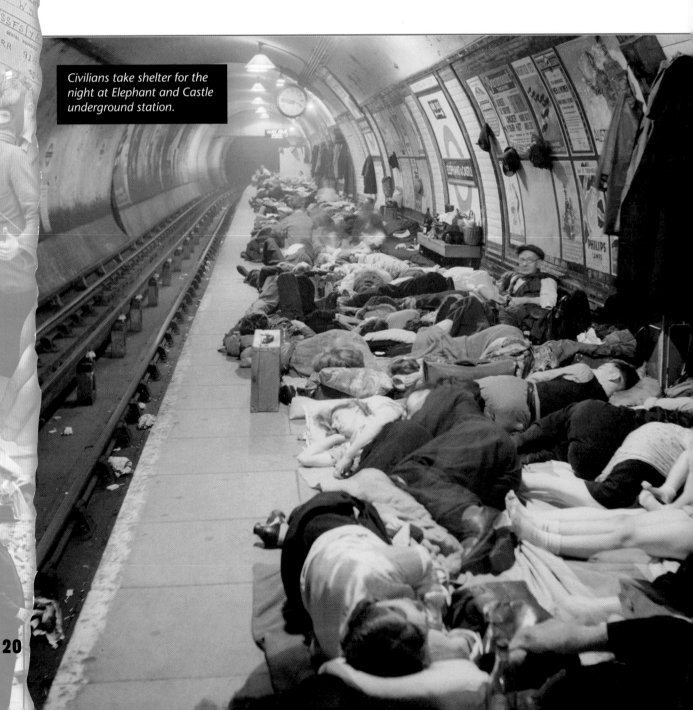

Civilians take shelter for the night at Elephant and Castle underground station.

Churchill inspects the damage after a bombing raid.

The medical student: Paul Lambah was a medical student living in London during the Blitz. He wrote a poem about the effect of German bombs on normal Londoners living 'in Civvy Street':

Civvy Street

Those first raids fell on the East End
Saw the Victorian order bend
As scores from other districts came
To help douse fires and worked the same
With homeless folk to help them flit
To underground that 'Wait-a-bit!'
In Government, had ruled out of bounds.
But bombing and those sights and sounds
Made common people take the law
In their own hands. The stress of war
And most of all their common sense
Ignored old 'Sitting-on-the-fence'.
They fled to tubes, the natural place
Of safety. Whereupon 'Save-face'
Made it official, issued passes,
Being thus instructed, by the masses.
Folk lived and slept in them in rows
While bombing lasted: through the throes.

The start of the bombing had a dramatic effect on the attitude of Londoners to each other.

Lambah felt the government had been indecisive during the war so far. He is probably referring to Home Secretary John Anderson in particular.

'Save-face' is another nick-name for the government who realised they could not stop people using the tubes as shelters and tried to avoid losing their authority by officially allowing it and regulating it with passes.

21

Jerry meanwhile turned bombers West.
He little knew that was the best
Action to take to unite us;
Once united to incite us.
Now Whitechapel and rich Mayfair
Had pretty well the same to bear
With other parts of our great city
Each in its turn. It wasn't pretty.
The streets and squares of bomb-wrecked homes
The broken spires and broken domes
All etched in deep with wounds and blood
Trickling to form a mortal flood.
A flood of blood, a flood of tears,
A flood of pain, a flood of fears

So night on night the bombers came
And little we could do to tame
Their storm of steel, their storm of fire;
Only lie doggo in the mire.

After the first raids on the East End, the German (Jerry) bombers concentrated on the richer districts to the west of the city, such as Mayfair. This helped to unite Londoners in a common cause against the Nazis.

Lambah feels the Blitz gave Londoners a sense of camaraderie with one another.

From 7 September onwards, London was bombed for 57 consecutive nights.

Life goes on for a family pet amid the rubble of what was once his home.

Lambah's neighbour remains cheerful after his house was bombed.

They stuck to it the darkness through
Working like Titans every crew.
In brick-dust stench, the hoses snaking
The land-mine's heave, the buildings shaking
The fractured mains, the lack of light
The sticks of bombs in screaming flight,
The belch of gas, the acrid smoke
The charred lump who was once a bloke.
The workmen's pluck, the firemen's grit
Forever in the thick of it.
The flare, the heat, the incendiary showers
The gaping pits where once were flowers.

The searchlight boys and girls their best
Efforts gave and though hard-pressed
A burning hate grew in our hearts
To beat the Germans; play our parts.

The police inspector: Evan Leslie 'Les' Williams was stationed at Balham, London, during the Blitz. He was quickly on the scene after Balham underground station was bombed in 1940:

" ...about 11pm I was visiting one of my stations when a little girl of about 11 years of age came in and said she had been in Balham underground station with her parents but could not find them and that they were not at their home.

Accompanied by one of my sergeants I went to the station. There were no lights and we only had our police torches to light our way. When we got down on to the platform and walked some distance along it we saw a huge mound of earth which nearly reached the roof. We could hear water running. We climbed up over the mound and had to slide on our stomachs until we finally got to the other side. We heard a rush of water and were both petrified. We searched for some time but could not find anybody...

What had happened was that a relatively small bomb had penetrated through to the up-platform of the station, exploded and burst the water mains and the sewers. The earth had been washed on to the platform and trapped the people who were sheltering there... About 100 people lost their lives. There was only one good thing about this whole incident; the little girl found her parents who were both alive and had themselves been trying to find their daughter. "

In the aftermath of the incident described above, a bus lies in the crater caused by the Balham bomb.

The British spirit

Over 41,000 civilians were killed and 137,000 injured during the Blitz, but the British resolve, inspired by Winston Churchill, was not weakened. Churchill believed that control of the Atlantic should be Britain's next priority, but to obtain that it would probably need America's help.

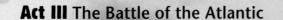

Pearl Harbor

Date: 7 December 1941

The USA had been doing a lot to help Britain whilst remaining neutral in the war – shipping supplies of food, fuel and munitions across the Atlantic. The majority of the American public, however, felt that the USA should not involve itself in what they thought was a European conflict, so President Franklin Roosevelt's actions had to appear officially neutral. That changed on 7 December 1941, when the Japanese launched a surprise air attack on Pearl Harbor, an American naval base in Hawaii.

President Roosevelt signs the declaration of war on Japan after the bombing of Pearl Harbor (above).

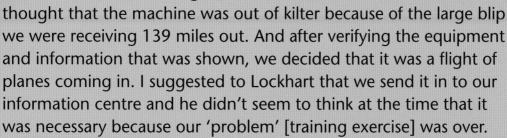
USS Shaw *explodes after the attack at Pearl Harbor.*

The radar operator: George E Elliott, a US naval radar operator, was working on a training exercise on the morning of the attack.

"   And of course it was just shortly after 7 am that we picked up this large flight of planes and Lockhart [a colleague] at that moment thought that the machine was out of kilter because of the large blip we were receiving 139 miles out. And after verifying the equipment and information that was shown, we decided that it was a flight of planes coming in. I suggested to Lockhart that we send it in to our information centre and he didn't seem to think at the time that it was necessary because our 'problem' [training exercise] was over.

But in any event we did send it in and sent the information in to Private MacDonald who was the switchboard operator at the information centre. And of course it being after 7, why everybody had left, the 'problem' being over. I left word with MacDonald, he said there was nobody there who could do anything about it, and I left word with him to see if he could find somebody who would know what to do and to call us back. And a little later why this Lieutenant Tyler called back and Lockhart answered the phone and in essence was told to forget it. And that was the beginning of Pearl Harbor.

I might add in defence of the man that told us to forget it – this was his first tour of duty, other than the orientation tour, at that location... "

The United States declares war

The following day President Roosevelt opened his speech to the nation, "Yesterday, December 7th, 1941 – a date which will live in infamy – the United States of America was suddenly and deliberately attacked by naval and air forces of the Empire of Japan." He concluded, "I ask that the Congress declare that since the unprovoked and dastardly attack by Japan on Sunday, December 7th, 1941, a state of war has existed between the United States and the Japanese Empire."

U-boats vs Convoys

Date: 4 – 5 May, 1943

U-boats caused serious problems for British shipping right from the start of the war. The British decided that sailing in convoy, with the Royal Navy protecting merchant ships, would be safer. By 1943 it was not going well for the convoys, with 120 ships sunk in March alone.

Britain faced the danger of mass starvation if the losses continued at such a high rate and the Royal Navy began to consider alternatives to the convoy system. Then, between 3 April and 24 May 1943, with the convoys HX-231, ONS-5 and SC-130, the tide turned.

Convoy escort vessels cross the Atlantic.

The naval officer: Robert Atkinson was the commanding officer of HMS *Pink*, part of the Royal Navy escort of convoy ONS-5. He relates what happened on 4-5 May:

"The convoy was split up due to bad weather and torpedoing. And I broke away with four ships and took them on my own. I couldn't catch up with the convoy. I'd rounded up four or five ships and I was proceeding to Newfoundland at the best speed I could, and the speed of a convoy was the speed of the slowest ship. Quite a long way to go.

Proceeding with my five ships I located an enemy submarine. Now in his book, Admiral Gretton said I made a mistake – my job was not to chase submarines, my job was to protect the convoys. But he said it was a human thing. Having got a contact, I'm the last man in the world to let go. So I attacked that submarine and sank him. And then having left my new convoy, because it took several hours, they were now miles ahead of me, unprotected.

So I set off at full speed to catch them up. My worst fears materialised. Just as I came up to the convoy, another ship was torpedoed out of my five, a ship called the *West Madaket*. I was sad, but I dropped depth charges all over the place, to keep them down and I saw the *West Madaket* lifeboats swing out and into the sea. Very tricky situation – there's a submarine lurking there, waiting for you to stop.

So by manoeuvring, stopping going astern, and all over the place, I suddenly came alongside the lifeboats. Lo and behold about 40 seamen, all with their suitcases packed in a lifeboat. Marvellous! The Chief gunner's mate said, 'Look sir, what d'you think of that lot? We're not going to stop for that are we?'

A naval gunner loads a shell on board a convoy escort vessel.

27

Crew members prepare depth charges to attack a U-boat in the North Atlantic.

I said, 'Tell them to come on board, but leave their luggage.' I said to the gunner's mate, when the boat was cast adrift with all the suitcases nicely packed, 'You want some machine gun practice?' 'Yes, sir.' The boat evaporated with the gunfire…

I said to the captain, 'Have you got your documents with you?' 'No.' 'Where are they?' 'Left them on the chart room table.' Panic. 'Well I'm afraid I'll have to sink the ship because she isn't sinking.'

She was torpedoed, but she hadn't sunk. So we steamed around again and with two or three depth charges we came close up one side, threw them under, broke her back and she went under in two or three minutes…

Later in life, looking up the records, and seeing the German records, the submarine that torpedoed the *West Madaket* claimed he'd sunk the *West Madaket*. I had an American professor over here doing research and he said he'd seen this man and met him. Would I like to meet him? I said I don't want to. Past chapter. I don't want to go to Germany and talk to anybody. But when you next see him, tell him, he didn't sink the *West Madaket*. I did. So I enjoyed that one.

However we claimed one U-boat and we lost one of our sheep and we got the other four back to harbour. That was my part in ONS-5.

U-boats defeated

Although Robert Atkinson was credited with a 'probably sunk' at the time for his attack on the U-boat, it has since been claimed that the U-boat in fact returned to base with severe but not critical damage. Despite this twist in the tale, Atkinson's story shows the changing tide in the battle against the U-boats. When Admiral Dönitz, the German naval commander, counted the cost of hunting these three convoys (15 boats sunk against 19 U-boats lost), he declared that the U-boats had been defeated and withdrew them. With the Atlantic secured, the Allies began to focus on how to take the war back to the Germans.

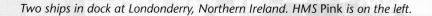

Two ships in dock at Londonderry, Northern Ireland. HMS Pink *is on the left.*

The Dambusters

Date: 17 May 1943

As 1943 progressed, the Allies stepped up their bombing of German civilian and industrial targets. A cunning bombing raid was planned by the Royal Air Force's 617 Squadron, which would destroy the German dams at Möhne, Eder, Sorpe and Ennepe. The raids were to use specially designed bombs to blow up the base of the dams. Huge floods would hit the surrounding industrial areas, slowing down the German economy.

A Lancaster bomber in flight (top) and an aerial photograph of the Eder Dam.

The RAF pilot: The leader of the Dambusters was Wing Commander Guy Gibson. Flight Lieutenant David John Shannon (right), another Dambuster pilot, recalls the raid on the Eder Dam:

> Well, the Eder Dam was not protected by any anti-aircraft defences at all. I think the Germans had thought that it was so difficult for anybody to deal with its natural surroundings that it was quite secure...
>
> Well I tried, I think four times to get down, dropping down, and each time I was not satisfied with the run that I'd made and told the bomb aimer not to release. And to get out of this predicament we had to immediately pull on full throttle and do a steep climbing turn to the right to avoid a vast rock face that was up in the front...

So Gibson said, 'Well have a rest of that, and call in Maudsley,' who was leader of the next flight to come along. And he had a dummy run at it, unsuccessful and did the same thing as I'd done. And then he did another dummy run and dropped his bomb, but the bomb overshot and bounced off the wall and again exploded. Below there was a tremendous flash. And we don't know what happened to Maudsley...

A 'bouncing bomb' in place under the fuselage of one of 617 Squadron's modified Lancaster aircraft.

So then Gibson told me to have another go, so I had another dummy run. And then I got what I thought was an excellent run down and we released the mine and as far as we could tell there was a small breach made on the port side, on the left hand side of the wall going through. But there was no significant sign there, and so there was only one aircraft left, that was Les Knight, and he was called up.

And he had three or four runs before he could release, and then he released his mine and.... the wall gave. So fortunately we were very lucky because that was the last of the nine aircraft. And that breached the Eder Dam. **"**

...and bouncing to the target.

Test photos of a practice run show bomb release...

After the raid

Although the squadron suffered heavy casualties, the Dambusters Raid was considered a great success and news of the daring strikes boosted British morale. In reality the dams were rebuilt much more quickly than had been predicted and German industry was less affected by the raid than had been anticipated. It was going to take a ground force to defeat the Nazis.

The D-Day Landings

Date: 5 – 6 June 1944

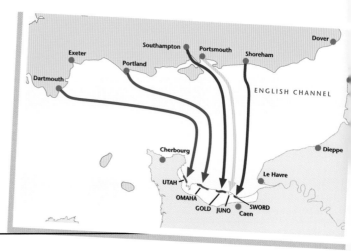

The American General Dwight Eisenhower became Supreme Allied Commander of the Allied Expeditionary Forces in December 1943 in order to command Operation Overlord – the Allies' return to France and the start of their advance to Germany. The timing of the Normandy landings (above) was crucial as bad weather could lead to catastrophic losses.

The RAF Chief Meteorological Officer:

In the run up to D-Day, Eisenhower tried to pin down the best date for the landings, as James Stagg, the RAF Chief Meteorological Officer relates:

"During those last days in May, General Eisenhower's forces were assembling round the south coast and up the west coast of these islands. So, most unfortunately, did the depressions in the Atlantic.

On the evening of Wednesday, 31st of May, even then, I advised General Eisenhower that conditions for the oncoming weekend, especially over Sunday night and Monday morning, the crucial time for Overlord, were going to be stormy. But we went on with the meetings. I had to go before General Eisenhower twice a day during those fateful days, 1st, 2nd and 3rd June. As time went on the seriousness of the whole situation got worse, until by Saturday night it became obvious that there would certainly be a storm in the Channel area on the Sunday night and Monday. General Eisenhower decided to halt the operation.

Prime Minister Churchill meets General Eisenhower to discuss plans for Operation Overlord.

Sunday 4th June was a day of dreadful tension. The whole operation was hung up. Our chart gave no indication whatever that there could be any respite from the storms for many days ahead...

Then, mercifully, the almost unbelievable happened about midday on that Sunday. We spotted, from a report from the Atlantic, that there might be an interlude between two depressions moving towards Ireland and therefore ultimately in to the south-west approaches. If that interlude could be long enough and if it arrived in the Channel at the proper time, it might just let the thing get started again. I convinced General Eisenhower and his Commanders that it would indeed arrive later on Monday after the storm of Sunday night, continue through Tuesday and probably into Wednesday.

The next morning, early on the 5th of June, they met again to confirm this decision and when I could tell them that we were even more confident than we had been the previous night that the quieter interlude would indeed come along, the joy on the faces of the Supreme Commander and his Commanders after the deep gloom of the preceding days was a marvel to behold.

Allied troops wade ashore from their landing craft on D-Day.

D-Day arrives

During the early morning of 6 June 1944, almost 150,000 Allied troops landed at various beaches in German-occupied Normandy. The Germans were taken by surprise. They soon recovered, however, and the Allies suffered 10,000 casualties while establishing themselves on the mainland. Nevertheless it was a momentous day for the Allies – the start of the final push to Berlin. But much vicious fighting lay ahead; not least on the Eastern Front, where the Russian Red Army was starting to advance towards Germany.

Belsen Liberated

Date: 15 April 1945

Liberated women prisoners burn clothes at the Bergen-Belsen concentration camp, 17-18 April 1945.

As the Allies advanced towards Germany, they began to uncover evidence of Nazi atrocities – the systematic murder of European Jews that has become known as the Holocaust. The first concentration/extermination camp was discovered by Soviet troops at Majdanek on 23 July 1944. Then came Auschwitz and Buchenwald in January and April 1945. The first concentration camp liberated by British and Canadian troops – on 15 April 1945 – was called Bergen-Belsen. The sights that greeted the Allied soldiers were truly horrifying.

The war photographer: A N Midgley was a photographer with Army no. 5 Unit. He arrived at the Bergen-Belsen camp on 15 April, took photographs and wrote this account:

> Some of the huts were marked with a red cross. Inside the scene was indescribable. I looked in through the window. It was impossible to walk inside without walking on the people who were in a dreadful state, more dead than alive. Many too weak to lift their hands. There were dead lying between the living – the living were too weak to remove them. Many must have died from suffocation, due to the overcrowding.
>
> Outside, dying lay beside the dead. Others burnt the shoes and clothing of the dead to keep warm. There was a huge pile of boots and shoes from dead people.
>
> At another part of the camp our soldiers had started to organise the removal of piles of dead for burial. They had rounded up several SS men who were caught at the camp and had been there as guards. They were made to load lorries with bodies. They were kept on the move by our soldiers picking up bodies from a heap and throwing them unceremoniously onto the trucks. The other inmates were loading, booing and shouting and throwing stones at the SS thugs. When the trucks were loaded the SS men were made to jump on top of the pile of bodies and the trucks drove off to the burial place.

Former guards are made to load the bodies of dead prisoners onto a lorry for burial.

On one of those trips, one SS man jumped off and ran away. He only got a short distance – he was shot dead by a rain of bullets to the cheers of the crowd. The SS men were really being broken down – some cried and sobbed as they were rushed about in their horrible task of picking up the corpses.

We came across a woman who claimed to be a British subject – her father was English, mother Belgian. She spoke perfect English. She arrived at the camp a few weeks ago, having been marched from Hannover – 40 miles away. They were without water for five days. She was quite [chirpy] and so pleased to know that she would soon be in good hands...

The majority of the people in the camp were professional, well-educated people. When the Brigadier asked for doctors, a large number of men and women stepped out. We were told that it will be possible to save many of the people but thousands are beyond hope and will surely die.

A starving woman near to death lies out in the open air.

Scores are dying every day. Food is now being supplied by the army but is not much good at the moment, as the people have been so long without food, solid food, that their stomachs can't cope with it. Milk is now being supplied and this they can take. One wiry woman clutching a baby appealed to the soldier in charge of the milk for a supply for her baby. He gave her a tin. She asked him to hold the baby and she bent down and kissed his boots. He looked at the child and soon saw that it had been dead for some time. He gave it back to her and she walked off clutching it to her breast.

We later saw and photographed the SS Camp Commandant Josef Kramer. When our troops arrived at the camp, he met them resplendent in his uniform, full of arrogance...

The people had been herded here to be systematically starved to death. No attempt was made to bury the dead immediately. Most have been lying in the huts amongst the living for weeks and weeks. And the living were too weak and demented to do anything about it. I have read about such camps as this, but never realised what it was really like. It must be seen to be believed. **"**

The camp commandant SS Hauptsturmfuhrer Josef Kramer, known as the 'Beast of Belsen', under British guard after the capture of the camp. Kramer was later sentenced to death.

The Holocaust

About 50,000 people died at Belsen between 1943 and 1945; there were many other concentration camps. It is estimated that in total six million Jews were deliberately exterminated on Hitler's orders. The following is a poem attributed to the German, anti-Nazi Pastor Martin Niemöller, about how the Holocaust was allowed to happen in Germany:

> In Germany, they came first for the Communists,
>   And I didn't speak up because I wasn't a Communist;
>
> And then they came for the trade unionists,
>   And I didn't speak up because I wasn't a trade unionist;
>
> And then they came for the Jews,
>   And I didn't speak up because I wasn't a Jew;
>
> And then . . . they came for me . . .
>   And by that time there was no one left to speak up.

VE Day

Date: 8 May 1945

The Allied advance continued through Germany to Berlin. Hitler committed suicide in his bunker and Germany signed an unconditional surrender on 7 May 1945, which was ratified the next day in Berlin. On 8 May, Londoners flocked to Trafalgar Square and Buckingham Palace to celebrate with Winston Churchill and the Royal family. Not everyone could make it to London but celebrations took place all over the country, in theory at least!

The soldier: James Bellows, of 1st Battalion The Royal Hampshire Regiment, found himself in Helmsley, North Yorkshire for the VE Day celebrations:

"It suddenly come through in the night that Germany had capitulated. Well – the NAAFI girls and us, or some of us, went down to the village square at Helmsley to celebrate. And what a celebration that was – there was nobody there! Only us, a vicar, his curate and about one other person. One of the lads had brought down a two-inch mortar with a load of flares, parachute flares. And he was putting those in and firing them up in the air. Suddenly a woman pokes her head out of a window and says, 'Why can't you be quiet out there?'

'We're celebrating the end of the war!'
'I couldn't care less. My husband's got to go to work in the morning.'

That done it. They went round, they tore the gates off, they... got the beer barrels and they lit a big fire in the square with all the gates and beer barrels and everything else. The vicar, he said it serves them right. He was all for it. No one turned out from that village that night. They'd had, I think, one man slightly wounded, and that one aircraft that had flown over, that was all they'd known about the war. By god, did we feel disgusted. And that vicar he said, 'Sunday, when they come to church tomorrow, am I going to tell them!'

***

Counselling for war – I've never had counselling, none of my mates have had counselling. But, my wife will tell you, there's no way when I go to bed that I can go to sleep and put my arm around my wife, because suddenly I'll hear a banger and pull her to me in my sleep. And I sometimes live different episodes of the war and I've got to overcome it, I overcome it myself. You still live it. You can't forget it. It was part of our life.

... the day after D-Day, we had reinforcements, because as fast as men was knocked out, you tried to fill the gaps. One lad comes and the job they had to do was collect the dead ready for burial. What happens? His twin brother was one of the first ones he went to pick up. Straight back to England. That lad was shattered. Those sort of things – you don't forget them, they happened.

But what I can't understand is all these people who've had five minutes of war and they need special counselling...

Children celebrate VE Day.

Post-war Europe

The war in Europe was won, but fighting continued in the Far East. The effects of the war in Europe were also far from over. Food shortages continued for almost a decade and loans that Britain took from the USA and Canada during the war were not paid back in full until 2007.

Crowds in Whitehall, London, during the commemorations to mark the 60th anniversary of VE Day in 2005.

The Atomic Age

Date: 6 August 1945

In the Far East the Allies continued fighting against Japan. In early 1945, US forces captured two important islands, Iwo Jima and Okinawa. The Japanese were also fighting the British in south-east Asia. But Japan's rulers still refused to surrender. On 6 August 1944, the US Government decided to drop their newly-developed atomic bomb on the Japanese city of Hiroshima.

The pilot: Colonel Paul Tibbets flew the B-29 bomber, 'Enola Gay', which dropped the atomic bomb. He wrote this account:

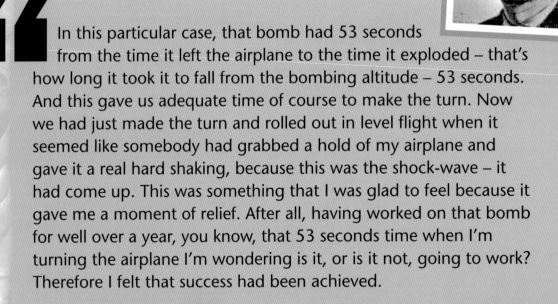

" In this particular case, that bomb had 53 seconds from the time it left the airplane to the time it exploded – that's how long it took it to fall from the bombing altitude – 53 seconds. And this gave us adequate time of course to make the turn. Now we had just made the turn and rolled out in level flight when it seemed like somebody had grabbed a hold of my airplane and gave it a real hard shaking, because this was the shock-wave – it had come up. This was something that I was glad to feel because it gave me a moment of relief. After all, having worked on that bomb for well over a year, you know, that 53 seconds time when I'm turning the airplane I'm wondering is it, or is it not, going to work? Therefore I felt that success had been achieved.

Now after we had been hit by a second shock-wave, I decided we'll go back and take a look. Because each of us in these three aircraft had cameras that we were looking through the front part of the aircraft with to take pictures of what was transpiring in front of us.

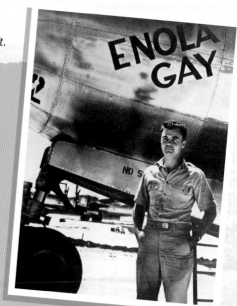
Col Tibbets and his aircraft.

The day was clear when we dropped that bomb. It was a clear sunshiny day and visibility was unrestricted. So as we came back round, again facing the direction of Hiroshima, we saw this cloud coming up, ... we were 33,000 feet at this time and the cloud was up there and continuing to go right on up. A boiling fashion. It was rolling and boiling. The surface was nothing but a black boiling... barrel of tar. We took pictures as rapidly as we could. My immediate concern after that was, 'It's time to get out of here.'

...I can't remember the exact phrase we used, but anyway, the words went back, basically to the effect that: the bombing conditions were clear, the target had been hit, the results were better than had been anticipated. And that message was sent on back. From there on it was just a proposition of letting everybody talk for a few minutes and get it all out of their system. The excitement was over. Pretty soon it became a pretty routine flight back home...

In retrospect, taking a look back, I do feel today that it's too bad something like this had to happen. But again, I guess there are many things in this world as we look back that did take place, that we say it's too bad that that had to happen. You can't turn the clock backward, you can't erase it. Let's hope that we did learn a good lesson from it and that we don't have to use it in the future.

"

The results; 'ground zero' at Hiroshima.

Japan surrenders

Japan did not surrender until a second atomic bomb was dropped on the city of Nagasaki the following week. At Hiroshima 70,000 were killed instantly. At Nagasaki more than 50,000 were killed instantly. Victory over Japan (VJ) Day was celebrated by the Allies on 15 August 1945.

Glossary

Acrid
strong and sharp

Allies
Britain and its Empire, the USA, USSR, France and China: the countries that fought against the Axis powers

Armistice
laying down of arms, a temporary peace

Atomic bomb
bomb using nuclear fission to release massive amounts of energy

Auxiliary Fire Service
an organisation formed in 1938 to support local fire brigades with their work

Axis powers
the name for countries allied to Nazi Germany – Italy, Japan and others

Billet
temporary accommodation, usually a military term

Black Market
an illegal market

Bren gun
light machine gun

Bren-carriers
a British military vehicle with crawler tracks

Charred
badly burned

Convoy
a collection of merchant ships with an escort of warships

Depression
in weather studies, an area of low air pressure which often brings rain

Depth charges
a bomb that explodes at a certain depth under water

Doggo
out of sight

Douse
to cover with liquid

Drifters
a type of fishing boat

Flare
a device used to illuminate the sky, or attract attention

Flit
to move along rapidly and erratically

Hitler, Adolf (1889-1945)
German Fascist dictator and leader of the Nazi (National Socialist) Party

Incendiary
designed to start fires, usually said of a certain type of bomb

Jerry
a British nickname for a German

Lower Saxony
a Länder, or state, of Germany

Luftwaffe
the German air force

Munitions
military supplies

Paddler
a type of boat

Panzer division
a German tank division

Pastor
a person authorised to conduct religious worship

Pluck
courage

RAF
the Royal Air Force

RAF Fighter Command
the military structure responsible
for organising the RAF during the
Battle of Britain

Squadron
a small unit of cavalry, aircraft or ships

Stokers
a labourer who tends fires

Throes
a hard or painful struggle

Titans
a family of giants in Greek mythology

Trawlers
a type of fishing boat

U-boats
German submarines

VE Day
Victory in Europe Day, 8 May 1945

VJ Day
Victory over Japan Day, 15 August 1945

Some useful websites

The Imperial War Museum's official website:

www.iwm.org.uk

Encyclopedic site about the Second World War:

www.spartacus.schoolnet.co.uk/2WW.htm

BBC history site about the Second World War:

www.bbc.co.uk/history/worldwars/wwtwo/

Note to parents and teachers:
Every effort has been made by the Publishers to ensure that the websites in this
book are suitable for children, that they are of the highest educational value,
and that they contain no inappropriate or offensive material. However, because
of the nature of the Internet, it is impossible to guarantee that the contents of
these sites will not be altered. We strongly advise that Internet access is
supervised by a responsible adult.

Index